It's Just Not Mother's Day!

Published in 2012 by Prion
an imprint of the Carlton Publishing Group
20 Mortimer Street
London W1T 3JW

10 9 8 7 6 5 4 3 2 1

ISBN 978-1-85375-834-8

A CIP catalogue record of this book can be obtained from the British Library.

Printed in Dubai

The publishers would like to thank the following sources for their kind permission to reproduce the pictures in this book.

Getty Images: /H Armstrong Roberts/Retrofile: 85; /Cornell Capa/Time & Life Pictures: 74; /Constance Bannister Corp.: 102; /A R Coster: 17; /Denis de Marney: 50; /Gerti Deutsch: 61; /Alfred Eisenstaedt/ Time & Life Pictures: 109; /Eliot Elisofon/Time & Life Pictures: 66; /Express: 41; /FPG: 73, 117; /Fox Photos: 21, 33, 37, 53; /J Gaiger: 34; /Gamma-Keystone: 110, 114; /General Photographic Agency: 58; /Hulton Archive: 6, 10, 22, 118, 121, 125; /Kurt Hutton: 9, 14, 18, 29; /Lambert: 26, 77, 93, 126; /Lapi/ Roger Violett: 81; /London Stereoscopic Company: 45; /George Marks: 86, 89, 128; /Ralph Morse/Time & Life Pictures: 65; /Joe Munroe/Time & Life Pictures: 69; /Orlando: 57; /A Y Owen/Time & Life Pictures: 98; /Popperfoto: 90, 94, 97; /Joe Schilling/Time & Life Pictures: 62; /Science & Society Picture Library: 105, 106; /Stockbyte: 78; /Topical Press Agency: 30, 46, 49; /William Vanderson: 42

Thinkstock: /BananaStock: 70, 113; /Comstock: 101; /Creatas: 25, 38; /Goodshoot: 54; /iStockphoto: 122; /Lifesize: 82; /Photodisc: 13

Every effort has been made to acknowledge correctly and contact the source and or copyright holder of each picture and Carlton Books Limited apologises for any unintentional errors or omissions, which will be corrected in future editions of this book.

It's Just Not Mother's Day!

The challenges of motherhood
caught on camera

Molly Miller

PRION

Introduction

Happy Mother's Day!

Flowers, chocolates, a lovely card and breakfast in bed…

Followed by 365 days of being taken for granted, as a nursemaid, taxi service, punch bag, unpaid psychiatric counsellor, not to mention cook, cleaner and personal lending bank!

A full-time job that would try the patience of the saintliest saint and all you get is one day's recognition a year? Well, thanks for nothing, greeting card companies!

This is a book for all the unappreciated Mums out there, who have brought little bundles of screaming mass-destruction into the world and somehow kept their sanity (well, some of it). To all the ladies who put food on the table and watch it disappear down ungrateful gullets; who wash and iron and encourage and nurture…day after day, after day.

When the sun goes down and the kids have finally found the Land of Nod, when you've massaged your partner's ego and provided sufficient physical affection to leave them snoring soundly, you might find yourself lying in the glow of the bedside lamp, thinking 'what the hell?'

Get a grip, woman! This is the perfect time to flick through this book and remind yourself that you're not alone. Millions of Mums across the world are sharing your pain. Makes you feel better already, doesn't it? Like your Mum before you, you've made your bed (obviously, no one else was going to) and you're lying in it, so your best option is to have a bloody good laugh, then try to get forty winks before a new day of domestic mayhem dawns.

Mother's Day. It's a load of crap really, isn't it?

Molly Miller, Mother

After three hours of swearing,
Dad finally got the TV
up on the wall.
Mum wondered when she
should mention that the screen
was upside down.

The war might have been over for years, but Mum still enjoyed a quiet night reading the ration books and nibbling on a bar of soap.

Irony (n). Attempting to save someone's life in such a way that they wish they were struck dead by lightning.

Peter liked being an only child,
so he used sleep deprivation
to ensure his parents would
never make love again.

Becky actually thought
head lice made pretty cool pets.

Many single Mums have to economise. Peggy bought a house without a front door.

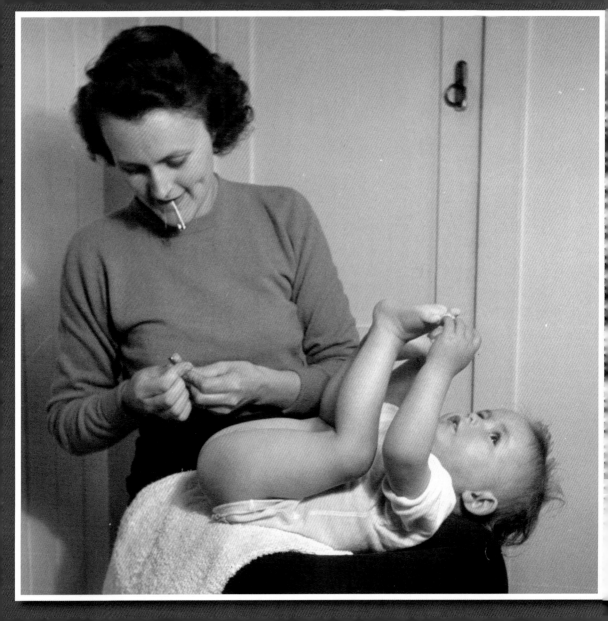

Little Billy's non-stop incontinence drove mum to desperate measures. But pinning his buttocks together would only postpone the inevitable.

Mum made sure the kids got
to school whatever the weather.

Dad complained that he
never got any attention.

Billy was happy to quality
control every item of furniture
that came into the house.
He knew Mum was grateful,
in her own way.

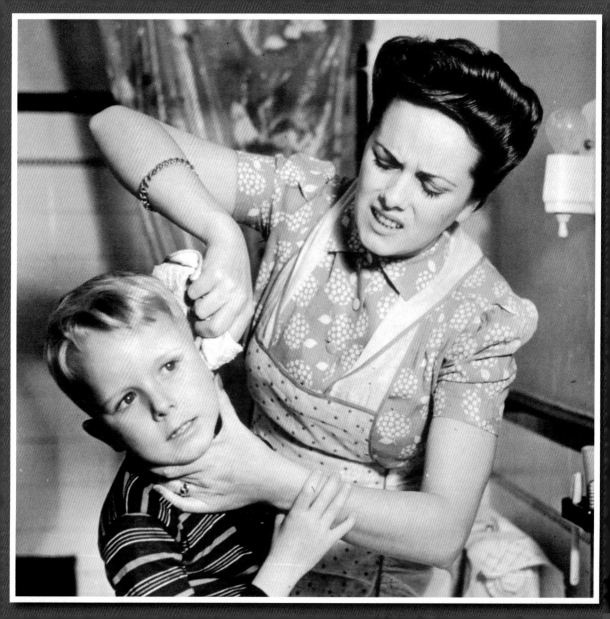

Wash time could be unpredictable. Like the time Jake put super-glue in the soap dispenser.

The local supermarket had a
'no-questions-asked' refund policy.
Mum decided to put it to the test.

Mum discovered that crab fishing wasn't too difficult after all.

After Wolfie ate Tilly's third pony, Mum realized they needed something more durable.

The 'off-road vehicle' was invented by Mrs Agnes Wetherby of Bromsgrove in 1918.

Mum would do anything to get the kids to sleep. The occasional bar-room punch-up or projectile vomiting session was a small price to pay.

Polly proudly showed Mom
what she had learned in school
today: how to fix a dislocated
shoulder.

Moving to Brixton wasn't that bad. You could always find someone to sell you some good sleeping pills.

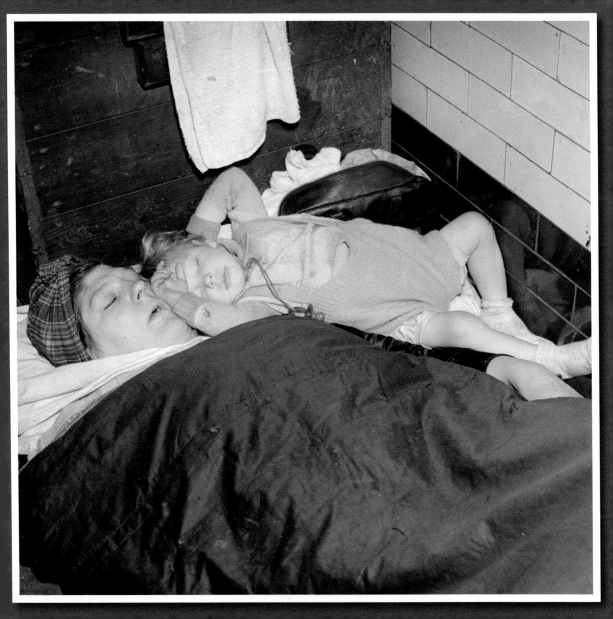

Before kissing Mum
goodnight, Jack decided to
have rabbit poo
for supper.

"The sooner you become a world-famous concert pianist, the sooner we can leave your father."

There was no 'naughty step' in the bungalow. So, Mum used Platform 3, Charing Cross Station.

It was Wendy's turn to
change baby Jon's nappy.

It was January 23 and
Mary was still traumatized
from seeing Mommy kissing
Santa Claus.

Mum tried her best to make learning the alphabet fun. Unfortunately Timmy had an acute fear of drowning and would never learn to read.

"There's obviously been some mistake! Don't you think I'd remember if I'd made 200 peak-time calls to Disneyland?"

Having a child prodigy can
be a mixed blessing. At just
2 years of age Donny had
already qualified as a dentist.
Unfortunately, he had yet
to master anaesthetics.

Mum said she could knit anything. Sadly Dad's crash helmet did not function as well as expected and the children were orphaned after a nasty collision on the M25.

Woodlouse paté was
Mum's specialty.

Some kids are just plain ungrateful: so what if the recent oil spillage had made the beach a bit sticky?

After much pleading and crying, Mum had finally persuaded Dad to get her one of those hi-tech washer-dryers.

Mum didn't believe in waste.
The leftover wool from Dad's
sweater tasted great with
tomato ketchup.

Robert's Mum grew tired of cleaning the dirt out of his ears and decided to grow lettuce in them instead.

The idea for filling the cushions with snooker balls had come from one of Dad's DVDs.

Gran said her special medicine was the secret to staying young. But Jimmy was not convinced - the wretched old crone was only thirty.

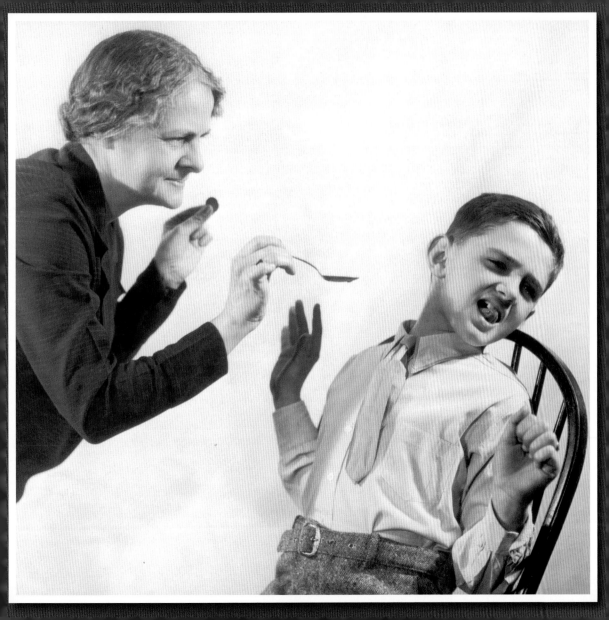

When her pepper-spray ran out, Mum climbed on a chair and waited for the police to arrive.

"Kids! I've set fire to the living room carpet, I'm leaving your Dad for an Italian footballer and, oh, your packed lunches are ready in the kitchen."

The kids outgrew their clothes
at an alarming rate until Mum
started injecting their shoes
with steroids.

Mum recalled something about
a '3-for-1 introductory offer'
at the fertility clinic.

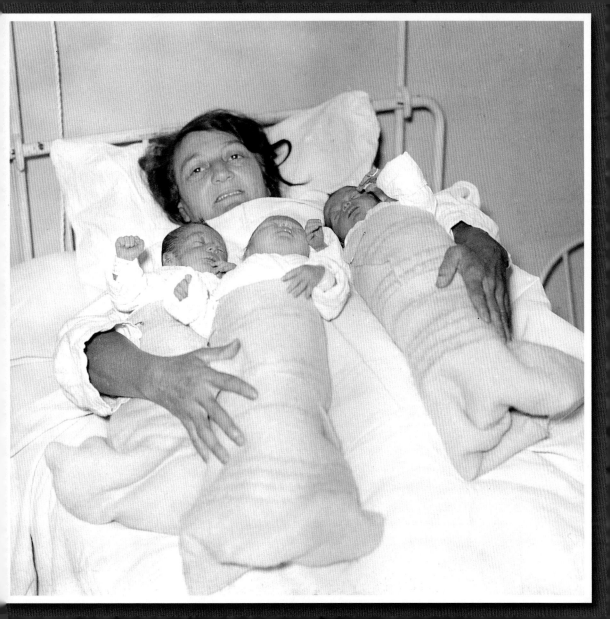

The doctor said Mum would be fine as long as she had no sudden shocks, or visits from cardboard velociraptors.

The whole family were equally impressed by Grandad's stories of fighting with the French Resistance.

They say that your hands give away your age. Now that she thought about it, maybe Mum *could* recall building Stonehenge.

The child benefit cheque could no longer keep Mum supplied with happy pills.

"Wait until your father gets home! He's going to be in so much trouble."

"Mummy, I'd rather eat my own hand than this disgusting muck!"

Mum couldn't afford to go to a spa, so the boys came up with something just as good.

"If you think this is terrifying, just wait until your first visit to the dentist."

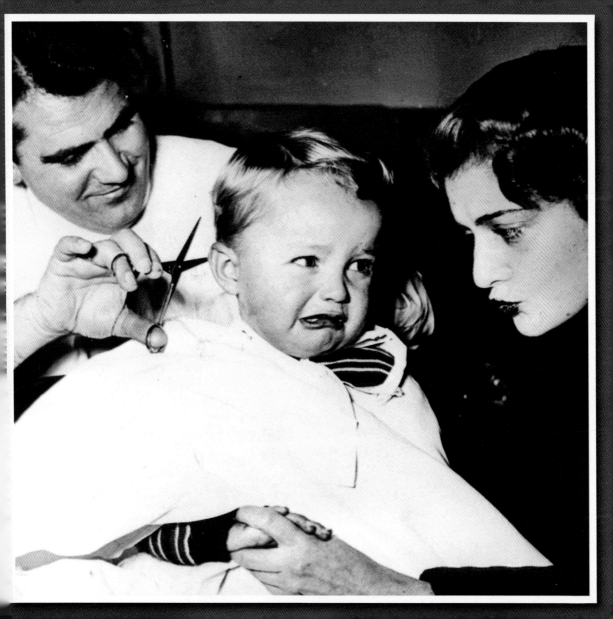

Screaming your lungs out is something humans have to do until they learn the F-word.

"Hello? Yes I need an ambulance. Four children are about to suffer horrific head injuries from a laptop computer."

Young Vidal had a few suggestions concerning Mum's latest hairstyle.

Dad's farts were really getting out of control.

"Gary, will you please stop
'high-fiving' your sister
in the face!"

Mum now wished she'd told
Emily that chlorinated water was
perfectly safe to drink.

When Dad turned up again after four years, Mum was furious. But it was okay, he only wanted custody of the kids.

Mandy was still at that
wonderful age where you sucked
at being dishonest.

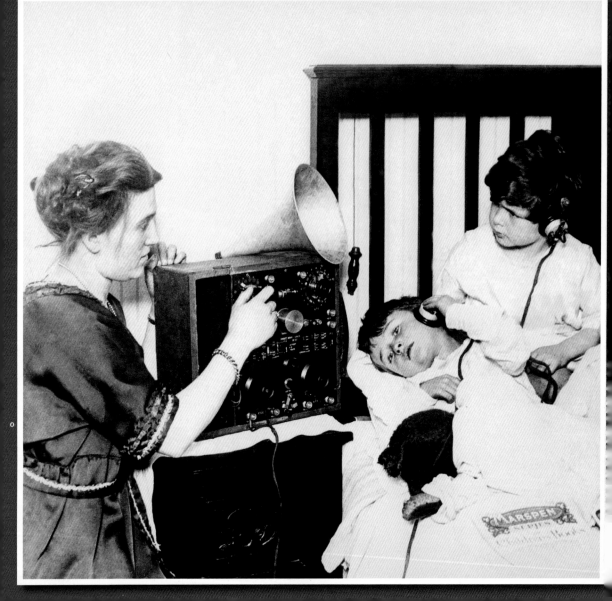

"Yes, of course it's an iPod.
Don't argue with Mummy or
I'll take it back to the shop."

Mum missed the kids.
But she sent them a letter
once a week from the
psychiatric clinic.

Charlotte was still having trouble dealing with Daddy's toupee, so Mum tried radical aversion therapy.

At just 4 years of age,
Harry had already decided
he wanted to pursue a career
as a serial killer.

Five forgettable minutes of 'passion', the world's ugliest wallpaper, and now a comatose lump whose snoring could raise the dead. Cinderella was going to have some harsh words with her Fairy Godmother.

'Deserters'.
The kids said they'd rather face
a firing squad than one of
Mum's desserts.

The idea for waterboarding
started life in Mrs Humberdyke's
bathroom, Finchley 1955.